TEN

YEARS AFTER

TIM PAGE

VIETNAM
TODAY

with 103 color
photographs

Introduction by
WILLIAM SHAWCROSS

ALFRED A. KNOPF
New York 1987

ACKNOWLEDGMENTS

Margie Collins at PAL (Philippine Airlines) guaranteed that I rode to and from Bangkok in style.

In Bangkok, Gary Burns, John McBeth, Geoff Goddard and many at the AP Bureau helped in and out egress.

In Ha Noi Australian Ambassador, Dick Bronowski provided advice and a haven from the storm.

Back in Britlag, all those who sat through the interminable hours of projection, thank you.

Hoa Binh

DEDICATION

In the spirit of Larry Burrows, and that of my mother, who ensured in me that honesty prevails. Let us also remember Neil Davis who guided so many through their post-war travails.

THIS IS A BORZOI BOOK
PUBLISHED BY ALFRED A. KNOPF, INC.

Published in the United States by Alfred A. Knopf, Inc., New York.

Distributed by Random House, Inc., New York.

Library of Congress Catalog Card Number 87-045353

ISBN 0-394-56464-2
ISBN 0-394-75654-1 pbk.

Manufactured in Hong Kong
First Edition

HALF-TITLE PAGE
Bomb craters in the paddies on the approach to Ha Noi Gia Lam Airport.

TITLE PAGE
Elephants walking from Ho'ville to Ha Noi pass the wreck of a T 54 Russian-built tank, destroyed during the 1972 offensive at Ai Tu, south of Quang Tri on "The street without joy."

THIS PAGE
Dawn rises over the coastal city of Nha Trang.

CONTENTS

Introduction

Ha Noi reminds me of Abbeville. Abbeville as it must have looked in about 1923, and not painted since. The same pretty villas with ornate ironworked balconies, steps and shutters. If the color of the stucco was still clear, it would be a sort of ochre. The shutters are all flaking green. The town is like a time capsule of 'twixt-war French bourgeois elegance, untouched by all the fighting which has dominated the lives of its citizens ever since the Japanese occupation of 1941.

The skies in Ha Noi are misty, grey and damp most of the year. Quite unlike the stinging brilliance of Saigon. (Saigon is more like Marseilles.) The different lights in the two capitals are very striking and you notice it at once when you fly from one to the other or when you take the Unification Express, the exquisite railway from Tonkin through Annam to Cochin, which has been almost rebuilt since the end of the war, and which gives three days of travelling the length of the war and the land. One can go further: the light reflects the political differences between the lives of the towns.

Ha Noi is lovely, but tired, dowdy and terribly, terribly poor. There are people sitting on boxes in the streets refilling the tubes of ballpoint pens and disposable lighters with hot syringes. (These are called Ho Boms.) Cigarettes (555s usually) are sold only one at a time—a pack costs a month's wages. Altogether, there is a feeling of exhaustion, of an immense task accomplished, but at enormous price, and only just.

The people of Saigon, Ho'ville to Page, are very poor also. But Ho Chi Minh Ville is still Saigon, still a sassy town, where the girls flounce around in bonnets and in the lovely flowing *ao dai*, the traditional dress; kids still screech up shouting, "Hi Mister, You Americenne?"; and all the world is in the black economy—just as during the war. Round the corner you can still change your dollars illegally—for about 400 percent more than what they give you in the bank. And your guide thinks you mad if you go anywhere near the bank. Everyone, especially officials, is still on the make and on the take in Saigon.

The streets are much emptier and cleaner now than during the war, much nicer too. The airport is a graveyard of old American helicopters, C 47s, C 130 transport planes and everything else which carried the war and the people, vainly, through the air for all those years.

But twelve years after the American defeat, Vietnam is still dominated by the war. The United States and its allies were driven out of Vietnam in 1975, but peace was not easily attained. Young Vietnamese boys are still drafted—this

An artillery officer on leave from the Chinese Front by the Petit Lac in Ha Noi.

7

time to fight on the Chinese front, a struggle which has been going on for most of a thousand years, and also in Cambodia for a buffer-state regime for which few of them care much. (Few Cambodians care for it either, though the regime the Vietnamese run – the People's Republic of Kampuchea – is far less brutal than the Khmer Rouge – Democratic Kampuchea – whom the Vietnamese overthrew in 1979.) At home, the North conquered the South, but reconciliation has not been easy, as the floods of boat people, now ebbing, demonstrated.

And yet, and yet, as Page found when he returned to Vietnam ten years after, the stark rigidities of the new communist government are softened by the easygoing nature of most of the Vietnamese. As I found when I was last there, Vietnam is, as it always was, a delightful, entrancing place to be.

It was from that trip that one of the notions of this book sprang. I was making a film of the Mekong River. We began in "Ho'ville" and went upstream on passenger ferries filled with goats and chickens and peasants on their way to market—a quite marvellous journey. One of my assiduous guides from Ha Noi, Mr Hong, suggested that I should soon come back and write a book to coincide with the tenth anniversary of the revolution. "I'd love to, Mr Hong," I said, "but I think it should be a picture book and I think Tim Page should take the pictures."

The Vietnamese liked that idea, but in the end they did not like my film. I complained too much about the secret policemen, made too many criticisms of their liberation-turned-occupation of Cambodia. They reconsidered the idea of my coming for the great big "Tenth Anniversary of the Liberation" bash of 1985, and rejected it. But they still wanted Page, the crazed Brit photographer who hitchhiked to Indochina in the mid-'60s, started fooling around with a borrowed camera, became a great photographer and had half his head filled with epoxy resin and covered with astroturf after having a great big hole blown into it back in 1969.

Page was different. The Vietnamese allowed him in before the rites and they allowed him to stay after the other boys had flown home. "Bac Si [Paramedic] Page, Professor Can Sa [Ganja or dope], Man with Hole in Head, who does the most famous anti-war book," they called him. And so he wandered stoned all over the country, as he did when he first went there in the '60s. His guides didn't seem to mind. Not everything had changed.

But a lot had, and this is apparent from Page's photographs. Compare them with those of his previous book, *Nam*. Instead of the clamor of war, we see now the pale drudgery of survival and the whisps of the past. The pictures here which struck me especially are that of the forlorn Cambodian elephant walking up "The street without joy," past a wrecked tank, towards Ha Noi, the lovely seaside town of Nha Trang emerging slowly from the mists, a poor woman in Saigon selling her pathetic possessions—kids' clothes, the family dishes, and two hens. There is the sad photograph of the refugees who, after immense hassle and many bribes, have finally got themselves onto the list of those allowed to depart legally. As they wait at the airport for their flight, their faces show their anxiety: will it really be much better out there in the West? For some, perhaps; but there are no guarantees.

Page will never get Vietnam out of what remains of his head. Nor will scores of thousands of other round eyes who worked or served there. I hope I do not, either. Though if it came to a choice, I would have to say that I prefer the far more easygoing nature of Cambodia to Vietnam. When I was making my film journey up the Mekong the contrast between the two countries was extraordinary. In Vietnam we were surrounded everywhere by plain-clothes policemen, nasty eager young men with sharp creases in their bellbottoms and sharper barks. Page was spared such surveillance, perhaps because he was not travelling with a film crew.

In Cambodia there were no policemen at all. Instead, in a little restaurant on the banks of the Mekong in Phnom Penh, I had Laughing Chicken Soup, or chicken cooked with marijuana. It took us hours to walk back from the river bank, through the curfew to the hotel.

But even in Vietnam the harshness of communism is softened by corruption. Most societies are corrupt. And corruption in Vietnam is nothing compared to that of, say, Thailand and the Philippines. It makes hard lives bearable; it does not make millionaires. As Page bounced around the country in a Russian jeep ten years after the end, he had almost as much fun as he did when he arrived there as a kid from '60s London. And there was the advantage that no one was dying for his fun.

Neither America nor Vietnam has recovered from the war. Why should they in ten years? Some of the residues of the war in both places are ugly. In America there is the Rambo mentality which is as ludicrous as it is repulsive. GIs have been compensated for their exposure to Agent Orange; the Vietnamese have not. In America there is the obsession with the MIAs, a great grief for thousands of families of course, but worth comparing with the hundreds of thousands of Vietnamese families who cannot even dream of the extended grief which American families can explore.

Every year we see old soldiers returning to Flanders fields and to Normandy beaches to remember their youths and their friends of the First and the Second World Wars. Nothing like that has happened for the GIs who served in Vietnam. Yet even a short visit to the stunning Vietnam memorial in Washington, its sheer black face echoingly engraved with the names of the Americans who died, shows the depth of feeling for Vietnam that still resounds through the hearts and minds of so many hundreds of thousands of veterans. To assuage the war they need to return. They need to go back to Khe Sanh, to Hamburger Hill, to the citadel in Hué, where the food is still the best in Vietnam, where (says Page) the girls are still the prettiest, and where I remember spending a night with my wife, Marina, in a sampan on the Perfumed River, while little children paddled out in small boats to sell us food and the hills shook with the roar of the B 52s bombing all around.

All those GIs need to go back to confront their memories, as Page was able to do. The version of Vietnam that they learned in the '60s was not right then and it is even less applicable today. Page's new book shows something of the spirit of the country now, poor as hell, recovering barely from the travails of the war, the countryside strategically dotted with the wreckage of a tank, an airplane, a patrol boat off which small boys catch fish and lobsters in the streams of the Mekong delta.

But they can't and they won't get there until that ugly-sounding but magic idea of "normalization" (of relations between the two countries) has succeeded. It seems absurd that twelve years after the end of the war the United States and Vietnam have still not been able to come to terms with each other. But they have not. There have been many reasons. Page is probably more sympathetic to the Vietnamese authorities than I am on many of these. I think the Vietnamese government is a cruel dictatorship and that its long refusal to compromise on its occupation of Cambodia after 1979 has been a pretty substantial stumbling block to restored normal relations with the United States, or its Southeast Asian neighbours. But now there are at last signs that the United States and Vietnam are inching closer together. Ha Noi is being more helpful in the search for the MIAs and an American office for the search for bodies has been opened in Ha Noi. Under the influence of Mikhail Gorbachev, there might be a deal on Cambodia.

When normalization does happen, the problems of Vietnam and the complexities of its relationship with America will not be resolved overnight. But understanding can begin. The United States can help rebuild Vietnam, and Russians ("Americans without dollars," as they are called) will not be the only long-nosed foreigners to be found pacing the streets of Saigon and Ha Noi. Then old GIs will not need to meet only in dives in Bangkok, as they do now. Like they did twenty years ago, they can fly in their platoons to Vietnam, this time in flowered shirts instead of khaki, as tourists not warriors. They can see and smell and breathe the exhilarating air of Vietnam, damp in Ha Noi, broiling in Saigon, in peace instead of war, meet their old enemies, and perhaps finally reconciliation not Rambo can be the toast of the day.

WILLIAM SHAWCROSS

There are only two forces that unite men—fear and interest

NAPOLEON

1 Unification Express

It takes three hours by plane, theoretically three days on the train, and an elephant can do it in three months. Ha Noi to Ho'ville, from the Red River delta in Tonkin to the Mekong/Saigon river estuaries in Cochin-China, a distance just shy of 1,250 miles, is one of the most beautiful journeys in the world.

The train journey costs 500 dong—a dollar or two on the black market—for one of the 62 couchettes "soft class", and 200 dong for one of the 642 "hard" seats. Trains are packed; one leaves Ha Noi daily, and one arrives. There is no restaurant car, but at every station where the train stops there are peoples' canteens, as well as private enterprise caterers. The State canteen has the liquor concession.

Taking the plane is more complicated. Booking must be done long in advance, flights are overbooked, passengers often stand at the back of the plane amongst unsecured baggage. You need clout to get a ticket and even then you or your luggage might get bumped; both are weighed at check-in. "In-flight" service is a negligible cup of green tea and one biscuit, no refills, and flights are rarely on time. Hang Khong Viet Nam, with its motley collection of one 707 and assorted Illuyshins and Tupolevs, has a track record in safety matched only by CAAC; flight still has the feeling of being on a wartime footing.

Our team was four-strong, including myself. Senior was "Ba Noi" (auntie) Luong, a short, wiry, intense, but alcoholic *ancien combatant* who'd seen forty years of military service. He had led a company at Dien Bien Phu and ridden the Ho Chi Minh Trail to the south nine times, once guiding the renowned Australian partisan writer Wilfred Burchett. Now he was assigned as a senior fixer to the Foreign Press centre in Ha Noi. My guide/interpreter/minder Le Tien had just finished his compulsory military service, with the rank of junior lieutenant, in the artillery up near Lang Son on the Chinese border. He thinks better English than he speaks, has a collection of 500 books in English, including Kesey and Kerouac. He quickly got hip to the nature of the project. Completing the team was driver Thuan, a scoundrel who was relieved of his job as chauffeur to the Moscow Embassy, after the Foreign Minister, Nyugen Co Thach, caught him with liquor on his breath at the wheel of his Volga Sedan. He was replaced for later trips by a driver who'd run the gauntlet down the trail to Khe Sanh, convoyed the Laos run and been rewarded with a drivership for three years in the East German Embassy – a thoroughly likable rogue and engineer/chauffeur called Thé, who filled the jeep with goods at every shop until we looked like a market-bound bus.

OVERLEAF
Southbound express nears the Ham Rong (Dragon's Jaw), a strategic bridge 2 miles north of Thanh Hoa. The U.S. lost nearly 70 planes destroying this vital link in the Ho Chi Minh Trail.

Our ex-U.S.A.F. crew bus
heads north out of Da Nang on
Route 1.

In addition to the A-team, we picked up guides at district or provincial
levels from the local Ministries of Information. In today's Vietnam, every province has a set of ministries duplicating the functions of its big brother in Ha
Noi. Without the permission of the respective committee, as well as that of the
military, Foreign Ministry and any other organization which considers itself
involved, constructive photography is impossible. It is virtually impossible to
climb into a rent-a-wreck and drive off into the sunset, clicking away at anything in view. Trips must be minutely planned – "programmed", as they are
wont to say, though programmes, like laws and bamboo, are there to be bent, to
accommodate the photo opportunities as the prevailing climate, temporary
arrests (nine in total), and mechanical delays dictate.

On the first end-to-end journey, we also ferried around the Director of the
Foreign Press department, Vinh Nam, a career technocrat with three years
service in Cuba, given to consuming vast quantities of Vietnamese yummies
and American cigarettes. A portly, middle-aged, polite nod-man, he had opened
unprogramable doors during his three-day hitchhike after the Tet celebrations
from his family home north of Tuy Hoa up to Da Nang.

We could sandwich up to eight people in among the gas drums, rice sacks,
camera gear and personal chattels. The front seat remained inviolately mine.

16

"Soft" class of the Ho'ville to Ha Noi express.

Bestowed somehow with the unofficial rank of "Colonel," I was described in the introductory passport that Tien carried as "a progressive radical photographic artist." This label was awarded to me by the Vice-Director of Press Activities, Duong Minh – an impassive diplomat who had served for three years as Second Secretary in the Thieu Embassy in London during the "peace" maneuvers of the early '70s: a true mole who had returned to his burrow. Duong Minh had given the green light on the book when I had reached Ha Noi in the Fall of '84 in the guise of a tourist. I'd stayed on after flying from Ha Noi to Da Nang, thence driving via Hué and Da Lat to Ho'ville for an extra eight days where I cruised the Delta, investigated the horrors of Agent Orange and re-education, and reconnoitered in depth to get a skeleton together for the book. It took 12 months and miles of telexes, cables and letters before the maze of bureaucracy was conquered, abetted from the Bangkok end by old media "Namy" Neil Davis of NBC, and by Little Thach of the Viet Embassy. We were into the big year for the Vietnamese, the tenth year of their liberation, the unification of the north and the south after forty years of maddened modern warfare.

Vietnam has always had allure; its name now has a magic ring in the lexicon of modern pop/rock protest songs, deriving from the vicious 10,000-a-day conflict, perpetrated during the American intervention of the '60s and

early '70s in what was, whatever they claim, a crazed civil war. I got caught up in the magic in February '65 when I deplaned from Laos as a staff photographer for UPI. By mid '69, when I was finally evacuated out, hemiplegic, I'd spent over three years based out of Saigon, gone on 150 operations, spent thousands of hours airborne and had been WIA five times. I had gone in at the deep end, loved the swimming and learned how to surf all over the pool. Asia was, and still is like a drug to me: Vietnam, the Ying and the Yang of total experience. The trials and traumas of recovery from the 105mm booby-trapped shell injuries back in '69 did not recede until 1980 when I returned as a tourist for 11 days, shooting for the *Observer* magazine. The Dragon was being chased again, without the combat.

Back in '72, when peace had been signed and the bells had rung worldwide, I had sat crying, listening to KRLA radio, suicidal, desperate, in a sleazy LA apartment, and had written in my diary that I wanted to be the first to ride the train of Unification.

The bombed-out cathedral in the centre of Dong Hoi, a strategic port city, once of 20,000 now of 5,000, in the panhandle of northern Vietnam on the Ho Chi Minh trail.

Hon Gai on Ha Long Bay. There are over 3,000 dolomitic islets here.

Little wonder that when the time came, my program requests ran like a Namstalgia jockey's choice of mounts: An Khe, Ben Tre, Khe Sanh, Ba Xoai, Bo Dup, the Fish-hook. The places where blood, sweat and tears had flowed, where ecstasies and agonies, fantasies and fears had been blown away. The very places that had made 'Nam one of the most wondrous places of my life, that evoked so much in so many other fellow-vets. The need to exorcize all those spots was still in gear. I had clutched at the fantasy of putting this book together for over a decade, and now it was to come true.

The backstreets of Ha Noi near the Long Binh bridge over the Red River.

OVERLEAF
Lang Co Bay on Route 1 between Da Nang and Hué. The blown bridge was the first major Viet Minh sabotage in '47.

Buffalo boy north of Hué.

Paddy fields near Ninh Lam,
north of Nha Trang.

The winning team in the first
Reunification Bicycle Race
from Ho'ville to Ha Noi—the
finish outside Ho's
mausoleum in Bac Dong
Square, on his birthday, the
19th May.

Two soldiers at Vinh railway station.

Back in the '60s, I had shot photos of several railroad minings, ridden two small sections of the track and been in one railroad/gas bowser wreck at Phu Bai. This time, I still didn't get to ride the rails. Even discovering a timetable was to provide a most daunting task that involved delving deep into the bureaucratic machinations of State-Secretdom. Spotting any train in the wilderness of Vietnam, where the tracks take off away from the coastal highway more than they parallel it, was complicated by abnormal delays that could drive even an old Asian hand to harder stuff. Where the tracks did parallel the highway, the problem was to get the driver to stop in time to obtain a good perspective of the trains. That invited instant arrest, though not forfeiture of film—just reprimand and more delay.

The station in Ha Noi still feels as if the B 52s are about to raid again: a glum, dirty, cinder-strewn expanse, from which emanates an air of Flanders on a wet wintry day. In between, the depots appear like sets out of a spaghetti western; some are raised platforms sandwiched between bomb craters, the result of the heaviest road and rail interdiction campaign ever waged against a transportation network. You pass through endless tracts of desolation under gradual restoration, followed by bays and beaches that shame tropical paradise posters, over paddies as lush as Asia can offer, and then plunge into primal forest jungle that would have enchanted Kipling.

The phoenix-shape land has it all; both the struggle to unite it, and its survival, seem mirrored in the length of that railway line.

All men are born free and with equal rights, and must always remain free and enjoy equal rights

THE DECLARATION OF RIGHTS, FRANCE, 1789

Statue of Ho in the war museum at Dien Bien Phu.

2 Bac Ho

I remember the first anti-war demonstrations in New York outside the Battery draft center in the Fall/winter of '67, when the protesters were chanting "Hey, Hey, L.B.J., how many kids did you kill today?" and "Ho, Ho, Ho Chi Minh." Vietcong flags fluttered in the autumn winds in downtown U.S.A. Che Guevara had been killed in Bolivia and raised to near saintdom by the new left, a hero of youth's revolution, the '60's look. Ho Chi Minh had almost achieved the same status. To the Vietnamese he was, and still is, the nearest thing to a god in a theoretically non-religious country. Saigon was renamed after him following liberation. The final offensive push also bore his name. He was loved, respected, revered, and finally embalmed and placed on solemn view in a Lenin-style mausoleum, built on Bac Dong Square in Ha Noi. He is a household icon, and offices, factories and hotels bear his portrait. When he was ailing in late '67, the party pushed for the Tet offensive of '68 to produce a total victory before Uncle Ho's death and 80th birthday. Death finally came before victory at 9.47 a.m. September 3rd, 1969, at just about the same time as the first anti-war moratorium was cascading over Washington D.C.

Image and myth blur Vietnam and Ho Chi Minh into one. Che achieved instant pop poster, hero status, though virtually unknown until being ambushed by Bolivian Rangers: Ho had already held that status for most Vietnamese for over forty years. He was 79 years old when he died, exhausted by the effort to unite the divided land. Always a nationalist first and a communist second, he was obliged to juggle the power of politics between the Bear and the Tiger, the Russians and the ever-noisome, age-old enemies on the northern borders, the Chinese.

Ho was born Nguyen Tat Thanh in 1890, in a small village 10 miles northwest of Vinh, a rice-farming community called Lang Sen. I made the pilgrimage out there, after overnighting at the officer's mess in a devastated, downtown Vinh. It took an hour and a half along a dyke-top road, a foot deep in viscous mud where road-widening operations were combined with filling in anti-aircraft positions and trenches. Vinh lies halfway between Ha Noi and the old DMZ (the 17th parallel), and had a burgeoning industrial output until it was blitzed and then suffered the final bombing of '72. I arrived in cold monsoon rain, which had left only a few farmers working their paddies. One is taken reverently to both the paternal and maternal homes, in adjacent hamlets. On this day these bamboo and thatch structures were mildewy, dank and

OVERLEAF
Ho Chi Minh's mausoleum, Ha Noi.

30

Place de l'Opèra, Hai Phong, the largest port.

The local committee of flower sellers in Ha Noi's market at Tet.

depressing, even to the guides. Ho's bed, his desk with pens, the hammock he was born in, his chest of drawers, the dining-table at which he ate, Ho associations *ad infinitum*—all emanating a glum air, all laboriously eulogized by a diminutive lady, who had to skip out of the neighbouring guardhouse in her tart shoes and best silk pantaloon, through the spreading puddles, to open up the

building for the worst-lit shoot I was to encounter. One of those days when the weather and the light made a clown grimace in pain. A dripping pilgrimage that produced a frame that feels shrine-like in a Japanese manner. The guest book revealed a paltry procession of Westerners over the years. Altogether an offbeat part of the Ho Trail.

Marshal Giap and his ADC. On
the left is Duong Minh, Vice-
Director of the Foreign Press
Centre. At the government
guest house, Ha Noi.

Ferrymen on the Son Giang
crossing north of Dong Hoi,
once a strategic link on the
Ho Chi Minh Trail.

OVERLEAF
A bus—an ex-Marine ¾-ton
truck—crossing the old Dac
Rong bridge on Route 9 to Khe
Sanh, the Ho Chi Minh Trail.

Ho Chi Minh's birthplace in
Lang Sen, 10 miles north-
west of Vinh.

**Tonkinese porterage bicycles
near Ninh Binh. These bikes
carried the north to victory,
carrying up to 500lbs apiece.**

The Quang Yen ferry on the
road from Hai Phong to Ha
Long Bay.

RIGHT
Bamboo rafts north of Thanh
Hoa. During the war these
pontoons formed bridges to
defeat the bombing
campaigns.

OVERLEAF
Under the Youth Union banner
in Cam Binh district between
Ha Noi and Hai Phong, an
understrength battalion of
infantry widen Route 5.

The descent of the Ho Chi Minh Trail had always loomed large in my fantasy-trips list, on a parallel with the ascent of Adams Peak in Sri Lanka, more a puja than an expedition, or the trek to Thang-Boche, the monastery at the foot of Everest. Few foreigners had done it, though in its heyday the Trail had reached B-road status, many stretches semi-paved, with truck parks, service depots, even gas stations fueled out of a pipeline that was eventually to run well over 3000 miles to just 60 miles north-west of Saigon. Back up on the Haute Plateau and further north towards the old DMZ, landslides and tropical erosion have completely devastated the tracks. In other places, Russian road engineers are jungle-busting a superhighway, which will tie in with the one descending the Mekong from Vientiane in Laos. Even in the years after the '71 peace talks, Cuban construction units had rebuilt the Dac Rong bridge on Route 9, and hacked a hard-top road down to the A-Lui valley, where there is now a large road camp. A memorial plaque to them stands at the spot where "grunts" of 3rd and 9th Marines had fought crack NVA regiments in elephant grass and dense scrub. A trip down the Trail today, grubbing off the beaten track, would take as long, if not longer, than when it was the lifeline of Ho's dream, Unification.

Ho Chi Minh's will, his charisma—like that which inspired the Americans under J.F.K.—produced the impossible, made his people tighten their belts to prison-camp standards and yet somehow enabled them to survive and win. There was to be no glorious crowning light at the end of America's tunnel and only a faint glow for the victors. Ho never saw victory, just envisioned it; Marshal Giap was to engineer it, and Le Duc Tho was to negotiate the finale. But the first of leaders lives on, through the Trail, the legendary sandals made from recycled tyres, and the city that was renamed after him on the second day of Liberation, so proclaimed on the old Saigon radio station. Bac Ho has entered the legendary hall of fame of revolutionary heroes; he was at the same time poet, militant, diplomat, and fighter. He was Uncle Ho, the one who enlightens. As his Premier, Pham Van Dong, said: "Uncle Ho is not dead, he will live forever with our mountains and our rivers, in our revolutionary cause, and in the hearts of our people."

A VC *ancien combatant* returns to where he fought during Tet '68, the summer palace at Thu Duc near Hué.

Money is coined liberty, and so it is ten times dearer to a man who is deprived of freedom. If money is jingling in his pocket, he is half consoled, even though he cannot spend it.

DOSTOEVSKY, *The House of the Dead,* 1862

3 Money-go-round

Money, just as it was during the war, has remained at best a farcical substance. Nothing has changed, though most Vietnamese suffer from a chronic shortage of it, the average per capita income being just under $300 p.a., one of the world's lowest. But then, it is difficult to measure the income of someone who gauges his wealth in simple possessions like a thermos or a bicycle, in a place where food is often scarce, if not rationed, so that the extra half-dozen eggs, bundle of sugar cane or branch of Tet flowering cherry blossom, bartered, spells a quantum leap in the standard of living.

Prior to Liberation, the piastre had been the prevailing currency, and it continued in use for 4 months after the fall of Saigon, until the new regime could distribute its hao and dong. The hao coins were the perfect recyclers' dream; people undergoing re-education dug up old American trash dumps, extracted the aluminium pop and beer cans, and the results were smelted down into light-weight slugs with a hole in the middle, similar to the old Indo-Tibetan coins used for doing the I Ching. Today, these pieces are almost extinct, worth more to a collector, and soon the lower denomination notes will follow, now that the dong has been devalued again.

Economically, Southeast Asia has been up the paddy creek for just about all of its modern history. The money sounds funny to start with: kip, piastre, kyat, baht, tical, riel and dong. All the currencies are soft and gauged against the granddaddy green dollar at often horrendously inflated black- or quasi-black-market rates. Then there is the free-market rate, the tourist rate, the trading rate: enough to confuse a fully fledged accountant. Things are worth more than money, especially in the newly liberated people's social democratic states of Indochina. After the Second World War, the currency in occupied countries of Europe became the cigarette. In Vietnam, State Express is now king, Marlboro and Salems queens (Salems, ironically, being ex-President Thieu's favorite smoke), and any other imported brand rates as royalty. Even a Laotian or Kampuchean "export" quality is deemed better than the locally made mixes, which are liberally offered to a visitor whenever he arrives in a new committee's domain. Each town and province has its own state tobacco and cigarette works, consuming locally farmed plants. Brands from one province will rarely

Selling pigs in Binh My,
between Long Xuyen and
Chau Doc on the Mekong.

be found outside that area, and then only on the black market: a cigarette pack collector's ecstasy.

Somehow the poorer and more socialistic a country is, the more the populace, especially the bureaucracy, seem to indulge in heavy smoking of blends that fall just short of pure bonfire but are incredibly expensive, a pack of filter tips costing the average weekly wage.

Most people are lucky to make 400 to 500 dong a month, about 1-2 dollars on the black market, which is the real purchasing indicator. A bottle of aspirins is worth $20, a bottle of Johnny Walker a Premier's yearly salary. Cap-sealed patent Western medicines are emptied, divided up and re-sold at astronomical sums. Though the state has one of the Third World's largest networks of health clinics, they are woefully ill-equipped with drugs; the aid sent them by both East and West finds it way to the black marketeers, often high-ranking party officials, not those for whom it is intended.

So go to Indochina, but be sure your grip is full of goodies to be distributed with programed largesse. During Tet festivities, it is surprising how many qualify for an obligatory present: ballpoint pens for anyone (a minor official must wear at least three); soap for Amasian kids on the Saigon streets (they re-sell it to bar girls and waitresses); Kodacolor film for province information chiefs; rock 'n' roll cassettes for hip guides/interpreters (Beatles, Abba, Dylan are No. 1); flashlights and sockets sets for drivers; T-shirts with any message (I've seen "Boycott Moscow '84" on one at a state fair).

Life in Ha Noi is the antithesis of the fat city, except at the foreign compounds, notably that of the Swedes, who have the largest capitalist mission, building pulp and paper mills that require the tearing down of yet more forest. The Aussies, who once had embassies in both North and South—10,000 troops, too—have the best bar and pool, the Billabong Club, and the most enlightened ambassador, who believes that Vietnam should be turned into an Asiatic Yugoslavia, socialistically non-aligned in the manner of Burma.

Among the Vietnamese, one has to recognize those who prefer Scotch, those with memories of the French who prefer Cognac, those who have children with a complaint requiring regular medication; and also the re-emergent unrepentant bourgeoisie, seeking tennis balls for use at the old Cercles Sportifs in the different southern cities. New balls are worth their weight in dong and the dour Tonkinese are finding it as hard to tame their southern cousins in peace as they did in war. Ha Noi, however, remains a city bereft of nighttime entertainment, street lights switching off at 10 p.m.

The labor used to farm the old free-fire zones and then turn them into habitable agricultural areas has a daunting task, for these places are still littered with an array of bits of unexploded ordnance. This makes human mine detectors of the people who are being persuaded into the new and better way of life and belief. The authorities at Con Thien, the old marine base hard on the DMZ, a key position in the McNamara line (named after the US Secretary of Defense who believed an enormous barricade of barbed wire and minefields could keep the North Vietnamese infiltrators out), speak of over 2,000 casualties, amputees and dead, and the clearing of nearly 17 million pieces of explosive, ranging from M 16 rounds to 15,000 lb. daisy-cutter bombs.

Despite the fact that there is so much reconstruction, that so much food has to be grown to keep abreast of one of the world's highest population growth curves, that the Vietnamese armed forces are the world's fourth largest, engaged on two fronts, in Kampuchea and on the Chinese border—despite all

OVERLEAF

Kids selling black-market
cigarettes on the ferry to Can
Tho.

Soup seller in the Hué
market.

51

The coffee shop's verandah
paved with 105 Howitzer shell
casings, on the perimeter of
the old U.S.M.C. base at Khe
Sanh.

**Recycling spent artillery
casings near the old U.S.
marine base of Chu Lai. Eight
dong per 100 shells.**

this, there is still massive unemployment, or under-employment: some sources claim as high as 40 percent. A worker needs to moonlight 2 or 3 jobs to make ends meet; peasants and farmers divert large portions of their produce to the free market. Goods on display on the State's store shelves are the only stock, the windows a pure fantasy of the unobtainable. No soap or shampoo, no toothpaste, much less toothbrushes. Vodka and cheap toys yes, gas stations no. Gas is purchased by the litre from roadside vendors, out of old Bière La Rue bottles.

Cyclo drivers await custom on the waterfront and Nguyen Hué Streets in Saigon.

RIGHT
A silhouette maker and his assistant, the Saigon Zoo.

It is the strangest thing to return to Bangkok and wander, as in an acid haze, down fully stocked, fluorescent-lit, garishly packaged aisles of giant department stores where everything is for sale, not just display, and where more is abundantly waiting outside to be bartered for. An hour and a half separates the divergent capitals; it could be oceans. There is an old peasant saying in the land of the Viets: "After the rain it will shine." Now that the currency has been changed, one new dong is worth ten old ones and new bills are being printed to cover discrepancies, but the rain isn't far away. As one glum E-blocer was overheard to say, "Ten old nothings equal one new nothing."

OVERLEAF
Recycled light bulbs at the Ha Noi flower market, Tet.

Ha Noi flower market.

Ha Noi flower market at Tet: 300 dong per peach branch.

Cleaning a drainage canal in
downtown Hai Phong.

Five-year-old co-operative flats occupied by teachers in Hon Gai.

OPPOSITE
**Women selling herbal
remedies and leaf vegetables
in Hué market.**

**Selling the family's
possessions for Tet, Ham
Nghi Street, Ho'ville.**

Victory is the greatest tragedy in the world, except for defeat

WELLINGTON, surveying the aftermath of the Battle of Waterloo

4 Namstalgia

It's not that Agent Orange leaves a nasty smell, like napalmed flesh, it's just that its victims, the children born to doused parents, tend to remind one of a cross between spiders and chimps that have been used for medical research. Agent Orange does horrific things to all living things—vegetation especially, which it kills. The motto of the C 123 squadrons flying the missions was: "We prevent forests." They called themselves ranch hands. The chemical's nickname came from the orange band painted on the 55-gallon drums it was shipped in. Great tracks of the countryside still look like the pox; grasses that should grow at least two yards in a year straggle up to two feet; fruit doesn't taste right. What Agent Orange has done to foetuses makes *Apocalypse Now* seem like a Disney movie. The insidious stuff, 245T chemical (commonly known as Dioxin), has been taken off the market for good in most First World nations. Meantime, Vietnam had 4.5 million acres defoliated—11 million gallons of Agent Orange in under six years, from mid-1965 to mid-1970.

The war was, from the U.S. side, conducted as much by machines as by men. The men were reduced too easily to computerized body counts to prove or disprove a winners'/losers' graph, conveying a sense of security, or aiding presidential credibility. "The American century foundered on the shoals of Vietnam," said a White House adviser, Daniel Bell. The conflict cost America a tidy 150 billion dollars and over 57,000 lives, now commemorated so soulfully, so beautifully on that slash of black marble by the Lincoln Memorial in downtown Washington, D.C. The Vietnamese lost at least two million people. Half a million are still unaccounted for.

The U.S. and its allies also left behind over 5 billion dollars worth of war goodies for the liberators. Much of it has been integrated into the gigantic forces of post-liberation Vietnam, but everywhere there are wrecks and ruins reminding you of the savagery of that epoch. At Ton San Nhut airport base, on the outskirts of Ho'ville, there is now an overgrown exotic garden for plane buffs. C 47s, the world's most stalwart transport, molder forlornly, undercarriages forever locked down, props adrift; C 130s lurch out of puddles; rows of Hueys, the taxi-cab choppers, stand lined up in a last desolate parade, their U.S., V.N.A.F. and N.V.N. rondelles overpainted, peeling bamboo pushing up amongst the few remaining rotor blades. Those birds came to be, more than anything, the symbol of Vietnam. There was always an unforgettable flapping mystery, a romantic thudding beat of expectancy to them. Sad and flightless, they line the apron outside giant peeling hangars, waiting for their final knackering.

OPPOSITE
Portrait of a VC: 53-year-old Va Van Long fought from 1947, making senior lieutenant by '75. Now Information Minister for Ben Tre Province.
BELOW
War museum, Ha Noi.

ÕNG PHÓNG LÔI
CỦA TÀU PHÓNG LÔI PHÂN ĐỘI 135 HẢI QUÂN ĐÃ
ĐÁNH ĐUỔI TÀU KHU TRỤC MA ĐỐC MỸ 2-8-1964.

ТОРПЕДОНОСИТЕЛЬ
ОН ПРИНАДЛЕЖИТ ТОРПЕДНОМУ КАТЕРУ 135ГО ПОДРАЗ-
ДЕЛЕНИЯ МОРСКОГО ВОЕННОГО ФЛОТА, КОТОРОЕ 2ГО АВГУ-
СТА 1964Г СТРЕЛО В БЕГСТВО АМЕРИКАНСКОГО КРЕИСЕРА
МЭДОКС

TORPEDE TUBE
BELONGING TO THE TORPEDO TUBE BOAT OF THE NAVY
135TH SECTION WHICH CHASED AWAY THE AMERICAN MADDOX
DESTROYER ON THE AUGUST 2ND 1964.

OVERLEAF
A captured U.S. M 48 from the '72 battles around Quang Tri reposes in the Le Ninh district near Dong Hoi. Abandoned for target practice—too heavy to ferry onwards.

Long Binh, the largest U.S. base in the country, stretched for miles; now it is a ghost town, the hootches and warehouses recycled, leaving acres of concrete foundation slabs. The main gate stands ajar to let locals pass to attempt to till the poor lateritic soil. Opposite are the VICASA (Viet Nam Steel rolling plant) mills. Gradually, all scrap comes here, or to a similar plant up north near Hai Duong. Tanks and shells, gun barrels and truck blocks all go into the same furnace, destined to be reinforcing rods and girders for reconstruction, or pig-iron ingots for export to Japan. Non-ferrous metals end up making fans and simple electrical appliances at a nearby Sanyo-built factory. There is no limit to the ingenuity the Vietnamese apply to the use of all this surplus junk, which may yet last for 20 years.

*   *   *

For me the hills still generated the same old spooky feeling; maybe it's the mists, the impenetrable, jungled ridgelines, the mountain folk—strange animistic vibes haunt the Haute Plateau, the hills of central Vietnam. I got lucky and was to drive inland from Qui Nhon on the Binh Dinh coast, with its magical riviera bays and vistas, to Play Cu over the Mang Yang Pass, and then south down Route 14 to Buon Me Thout. Route 14 is the main artery through the Plateau: whoever controlled it and the Mang Yang Pass could own the *cordillera* plantations of tea and coffee. After Play Cu the road goes on to Kampuchea and the Mekong. It bisects the Ho Chi Minh Trail at a number of points, before becoming a back door to Thailand.

Over the years, Route 14 has been the focus of intense military campaigns. My second field trip, in February '65, had been to the scene of an ambush of special forces west of An Khe, in the Mang Yang Pass. A convoy had been zapped at close range from tall elephant grass; we had come back three days later to sort out the bodies and wrecked vehicles. The Special Forces were expanding the perimeters of their B-team camp, heralding the eventual arrival, in late summer, of the 1st Air Cavalry division, with its 600 choppers, to build the biggest helipad in the world: it was to be called the Golf Course. The VC had chosen to spring the ambush at the exact spot on which their Viet Minh fathers had destroyed the famous French flying column GM 100 in June of '54. This had signalled the French evacuation of the region, and soon the whole of Vietnam, after the Armistice in August. Like an archaeological dig, decades of history sliced away at the gruesome site.

Confusion and my first taste of fear had been stroked that day: now it was difficult even to spot the place. The pass had been successfully defoliated and was still barren. The base of An Khe was deserted, though the weed-encrusted runway is occasionally used. Now the truck wrecks up the pass were Russian Gaz, or Chinese copies, not the big GMs and Fords of America's Red Ball highway to the hills. Strange not to feel apprehensive perched up in the Blue Max, trundling through boondocks where choppers went up to over 1500 feet, to stay out of range of Charlie's heavy machine-guns. Now it was his country and ambushes were out, although there were rumours through the security network that the insurgent FULRO movement, the front for the liberation of minority peoples, had been taking out E-blocers in jeeps with RPGs only six weeks previously. An ironic full circle for the foreigner.

An "irregular" trooper and his
girlfriend in a French bunker
atop the Hai Van Pass, north
of Da Nang.

The beach at Vung Tau, once
an incountry R&R centre for
Australian and U.S. troops.

OVERLEAF:
The remains of a B 52 shot
down on December 27th,
1972. Ngoc Ha suburb of Ha Noi.

Ambushed riverine Monitor
assault craft beached
downstream from Ben Tre on
the Mekong.

Camp Holloway, the first U.S. base to be heavily mortared in '64, causing retaliatory bombing of the north, was resplendent in flame trees, spreading over the old hootches and Quonset huts, which now house a Teacher Training College for the expanding immigrant population. The Montagnards had always been repressed by the Viets, and had taken to servitude under the French on their plantations, and to mercenary life under the American "saviours." The sparsely populated zone has now become the dumping ground for the over-populated cities of Tonkin. The local Montagnards are not as happy as they are made out to be. Their cousins, the Bru, who live further north around Khe Sanh, are virtually prisoners in a quasi-gulag centered on the old base, where they turn out cheap handicrafts.

I have the feeling that the Vietnamese are deliberately leaving strategic wrecks, bunkers and bases to rot for their future touristic merits. Why else is a large chunk of B 52 still stuck in a suburban Ha Noi duck pond, or Maginot-style bunker slabs left at the McNamara line, just south of the old DMZ? Any return-ing Frenchman or American can have his choice of relic to pick over, to stir the ashy reminders of past conflicts. Ghosts are revealed in the spring *crachin* mists over the strip of land between Dong Ha and Hué. Here were acres of

Nguyen Thi Ngoc Phoung, chief doctor of the Tu Du women's hospital, in the morgue of foetuses aborted due to Dioxin poisoning, Ho'ville.

AmAsian boy at the 10th Anniversary of Liberation parade, Ho'ville, April 30th, 1985.

fortified bases, embattled during the American epoch, and savaged over by north and south Viets during "Vietnamization," once the allies had departed with Nixon's trumped-up peace with honor.

A litter of shell casings spikes the sandy roadside tracts. Barbed wire, awaiting recycling, grows like tumbleweed. T 34s and T 54s, knocked out in the vicious '72 offensives by the new generation of chopper-mounted TOW missiles, the M 42s, are still parked where they ran out of track. Carcasses of trucks, cars, even forklifts, are strewn across the buckled plating of Ai Tu combat Air Base. Quang Tri is no longer. A mere 5,000 people eke out a living picking through the craters and rubble, slowly putting it back on the map. Even the old citadel, with its 20-foot walls, is grassed-over. Northern Europe in the early '50s. Desolation Row. The French called it *La rue sans joie.* For any vet war buff or historian, the battlefields are still there, almost maintained to a people's museum standard. Eventually, just as the last American flag in Vietnam was removed from the tailplane of a wrecked CIA Porter Pilatus at the TSN airplane graveyard with full media coverage, the debris of the wars will be recycled. Will those who were there heal their scars so well?

Anti-aircraft bunkers at the estuary of the Son Pha River, Vinh.

Destroyed U.S. M 48 tank, Marble Mountain, Da Nang.

Air America Porter Pilatus
STOL planes and Huey
choppers in the airplane
graveyard at Ton San Nhut
airbase, Ho'ville.

I saw, I saw, I saw holes and trenches
Full of the corpses of my brothers and sisters.
Mothers, clap for joy over war.
Sisters, clap and cheer for peace.
Everyone clap for vengeance.
Everyone clap instead of repentance.

TRINH CONG SON, after the Tet Offensive

5 Tales of the Dragon

Trinh Cong Son was the Dylan/Lennon poet laureate of 'Nam in the sixties. Today he continues to reflect that mood, if in a more suppressed way, and his work is as underground now as it was then. Hué, his native place, is the quintessence of this land. Here the emperors and mandarins built tombs, gardens, palaces—and the immense citadel that became the focus of the Tet Offensive of '68, when NVN and VC troops held out for twenty-five days against the tremendous odds rained on them by every weapon in the U.S. arsenal, short of the nuke. Now much of the city is rebuilt, though the ancient monuments and temples are still in need of massive restoration.

Hué still feels like the cultural fountainhead of Vietnam. It still bustles colorfully along the Perfume River. Tennis is still played on the courts of the Cercle Sportif on the south bank: profiteering committee middlemen leap about in an assortment of black-market sportif clothing and sneakers, brandishing hi-tech, mega-dong imported racquets where they once carried AK 47s and RPGs. A new market thrives, with a section devoted to recycled war goodies; an ammo box will cost you a dollar, and is guaranteed watertight. Next door a man squats on a GI poncho, trading the herbs, roots and powders that make up the traditional Ayurvedic medicines of the Orient. The past is back; the country has become more "Vietnamized" than it ever was in its modern history. The old ways and moral values have been re-assumed, veneered heavily with a communist doctrine, but one that is distinctly Vietnamese. Russians, communist or not, are simply Americans without dollars; the Chinese are the traditional enemies.

Traditional Tet dragon dance performed by youth troop in Ton San suburb of Ho'ville.

The Petit Lac, Ha Noi.

The saddest place, for me, was the Isle of Phoung, where the Daoist coconut peace sect held sway from the mid-'60s to the mid-'70s. Devoted to macrobiotic peace under its aged, celibate, ex-chemical-engineer guru, it had represented the confluence of all faiths and philosophies where a few of us had found ourselves in the midst of mayhem. It was like an oriental Disneyland to the passing freighter heading upstream along the Mekong to Cambodia, a quixotic pile of concrete, galleries and garishly painted sculptures depicting the mythologies of Cochin-China and of Southeast Asia at large.

The 5,000-plus devotees, clad in paddy Buddhist brown, lived on fruit and coconuts; they had trickled there from all sides of the war to pray, to live for peace. The Dao Dua, their leader, disappeared in 1974; in 1975, post-liberation, many of the hardcore monk peaceniks were re-educated, and the island sand-bar became overgrown with encroaching mangroves. Paint peeled off the concrete phoenixes, rust crazed the galleries and towers. The few people remaining carve chopsticks and spoons from the coconut palms which were once a part of the philosophy, for sale to the periodic clumping bodies of E-bloc tourists, or the sparser Australian or European mini-tour groups. Though the guru's body was never found, the islanders have erected the traditional funeral urn bearing his portrait.

Deeper into the Delta, all is still verdant, resplendent carpets of rice, interspersed with neat villages and those bamboo-tree lines that were omnipresent during the war, often harboring hidden machine-gun nests, communication trenches and bunkers, from where murderous fire could scythe at you as you plodded through the mire. Agriculture has been pseudo-privatized. Traditionally suspicious peasants loathed being collectivized, communized or coerced after years of absentee landlordism, bribery and corruption. Now, they must supply a quota to the local State organ; the rest they are able to trade on the free market, known as private enterprise. Southern towns, those south of the old DMZ, sport flourishing markets while State stores stand empty-shelved. Anything can be bought with a mound of dong: in Vietnam, there will always be a right price; before, it was just the same mound equated in piastres.

Canals still intersect the vast rice fields, the old highways of Cochin feeding to one of the greatest rivers of the world, the Mekong, the artery of Asia, stretching right back up into Tibet. President Johnson had held a carrot of peace out to Ho Chi Minh, in the belief that he could make him an offer he could not refuse: 100 million dollars into the Mekong Development Fund. Reunification meant more to Uncle Ho and the comrades. Today the militant Hoa Hao sect has been squeezed onto a large alluvial island, hard on the Kampuchean river frontier, where they still control the river traffic and own the richest farmland in the country. Most people are encouraged to tune in religiously to the new People's State Palace of Religion, a hideous establishment plonked down on an ancient Khmer site on the border, plagued by beggars and armed guards. It was in this corner of the country that Pol Pot's Khmer Rouge ran amok for a week, slaughtering thousands and giving the Vietnamese the ignition key for their invasion of Kampuchea in late '78. Smuggling and piracy, the classic *modus vivendi* hereabouts, flourish cross-border, as of old, normally under the watchful eye of fortified State farms, Indo-Chinese kibbutzim.

*　　*　　*

Pilgrims on their way to
Huong Son mountain for
traditional fertility rites.

On the banks of the Perfume River, Hué.

A Lao girl awaits a lift back home at the Cam Lo/Con Thien junction on Route 9.

The Cao Dai temple, Tay Ninh.

Lighting incense *(huong)* on
his father's grave, The
Liberation Fighters
Cemetery, Xuan Loc.

Ha Noi cathedral.

The ossuary of 2,500 massacred by Pol Pot troops on 22nd April, 1978, Ba Chuc on the Kampuchean border.

Sundays in Saigon. The heart of the new Ho Chi Minh Ville finds the French-built cathedral full for Mass, a saddened crowd seeking solace at the cross, conducted by a tame bishop. The religious hierarchy still exists, but to become a priest, bikkhu or imam, you must now take a philosophy degree at a State University before entering the seminary of your religious persuasion. Getting into a university depends on who you are, what you were and how the system sees you: Big Brother appraises the students meticulously. Believing in things outside the State is not encouraged; practising one's beliefs is becoming increasingly difficult. Yet the Montagnards still animistically drink their way through gallons of fermented rice wine *(shum)* to a secret paradise, which they would prefer to be uninhabited by any lowlanders; truck drivers still place Huong (joss sticks) on roadside altars to placate ancient spirits; beggars cluster at tourist spots, guaranteed traditional alms. The Cao Dai in Tay Ninh, 60 miles from Ho'ville on the Kampuchean border, who feature as the Third Force in *The Quiet American* (one of the few English books translated into Vietnamese), maintain their Pope, retired, and their Papal See and outrageous Vatican. There are still 75,000 practitioners; this is a force that no one has ever wanted to alienate. They sit on the gate to Kampuchea.

Everyone, nuns and monks included, dutifully waves red flags at the regimented Liberation Day Parade, but the traditional mores have come back into play. We have only known this place during its hiatus, at the peak of its pain, during the war; few of us saw its softer side. Now, after the dusty communist cover is brushed aside, the pastels glow through. An occasional *ao dai*, the traditional Vietnamese dress, floats by.

Mother and daughter outside
the Central Market, Ho'ville,
Tet.

A wandering Buddhist monk,
downtown Ho'ville.

OPPOSITE
**Rhadé drinking *shum* near
Buon Me Thuot.**

**Rowing sugar cane to market,
Long Thanh canal, southwest
of Can Tho.**

The view from A1 (Elaine to the French) outpost, of the battle plan of Dien Bien Phu.

155mm howitzer on the Dien Bien Phu battlefield.

Yankee, I swear to you
with words as sharp as knives
Here in Vietnam it is either you or me
And I am already here
So you must go.

'66 LIBERATION FRONT SONG

6 | *Liberation*

There is an old peasant saying that if a son is mistreated by his father, he may adopt another. The Vietnam saga is a series of liberations going back a millennium. The last episode against the Americans' neo-colonialist spasm ended on April 30th, 1975, when tank no. 844—a Russian-built T 54 that had trundled over 2,000 miles down the Ho Chi Minh Trail from Ha Noi—broke through the Presidential Palace gates (that is, after its Tonkinese crew had stopped to ask for directions.) The Palace stands at the end of Thong Nhut Boulevard, 500 yards or so past the old U.S. Embassy, which has now become the seat of the Oil & Gas Ministry for the offshore fields discovered in the last years of the southern Republic.

In April/May of '85, the U.S. was back, buying time again, but for television: instant replay of the unfathomable conscience. The NBC *Today* shows were beaming "live," via satellite, the tenth-anniversary celebratory throes of Victory, Unification, and Liberation. Celebration parades had been programed in most southern cities, but not on the scale that TV and Hollywood—and dollars—demanded, so the country geared up for an invasion of a light battalion of media, with the climax in Ho'ville. Also in the picture was a Russian film crew, shooting a feature-length co-production with the Vietnamese on the history of the war. The episode at hand, "Saigon Commando," featured Russian sailors, youth Komsomols, tourists and E-bloc hippies cast as GIs, and even Hong Kong cops. Anglo-Chinese-style billboards and signs unconvincingly tried to persuade audiences back home in the USSR that the streets of Saigon were actually downtown Wan Chai. Little was done to divert Ho Chi Minh tourist buses from being part of the *mise en scène,* much less explain the lack of skyscrapers along the Saigon river.

OVERLEAF
Blind, pensionless, old regime soldier, begging outside Buon Me Thuot cathedral after Sunday mass.

Desecrated ARVN graves at the former military cemetery, Long Binh.

The airplane graveyard at Ton San Nhut airbase.

OVERLEAF
Dawn on Route 14, between Buon Me Thuot and Play Cu.

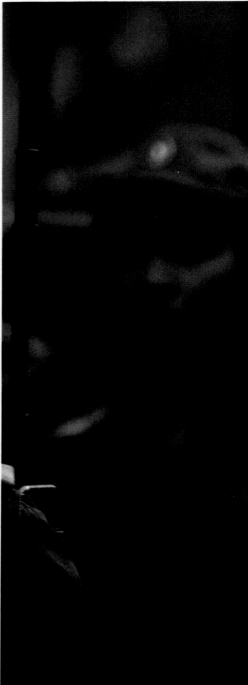

Billboard extolling co-operation between Viet, Lao and Khmer women, Buon Me Thuot.

**Women's signal corps march
in the 10th Anniversary of
Liberation parade, Ho'ville.**

OVERLEAF
**Buddhist delegation passes
the review stand, 10th
Anniversary of Liberation
parade.**

A media battle ensued. The old hard core from the war days had gathered for a final assault. Four U.S. networks, the Japanese, Brits, Aussies, Dutch, Swedes, *et al.,* wanted a chunk of the Telecom dish in the grounds of the old Presidential Palace; otherwise you had to bird out via Lotus II, a satellite station in the suburbs, run by the Russians relaying via Ha Noi and Moscow. ABC went that way. The mass of press created a zoo, uncontrollable even by the minders

and ministers. We became the event. Places hitherto off-limits flew welcome banners vying for the exposure, a notch up the proletariat ladder. Later, after the circus, it all went back quickly out of bounds. The whole system had burnt out at one party—Namstalgia abated. Most of us had been there to probe America's conscience, all of us had been there to find out why we'd been there.

Ironically, Europe was in the midst of its own liberation celebrations. It was 40 years since VE Day and Reagan was compounding his dilemma by visiting SS war cemeteries, then Belsen, causing endless consternation on all sides. There were no American diplomats on the review stand in Ho'ville, just lots of over-stuffed and sweating Ambassadors from COMECON and fraternal countries, plus a series of be-medalled, aged heroes of the Revolution now demoted to re-educated yes-men with no say in the Tonkinese-run way of things. Winners, losers, the roles all reversed. Somehow the powers-that-be had got it wrong. The dignitaries had to sit in the full glare of the new day, the sun in their eyes, until they were finally issued with identical panama hats. The media, though herded into an ever-decreasing patch in front of the band opposite, were shaded by the tall plane-trees planted during the days when Saigon had been the Pearl, the Paris of the East. Finally, after most of the military hardware and troops had dutifully paraded by and we were reduced to an endless passage of ministerial floats, young pioneers and religious groups, all flourishing scarves and little yellow-starred red flags, all vaguely out of sync, the crowd got its revenge by surging forward from the shaded footpaths to encroach on the columns, funneling them into an ever-narrowing stream. Security troops waded into the masses with bamboo Lahtis. Diminutive parading schoolchildren jostled with the rough crowd. Dancers' choreographies became a disco confusion. The press stampeded to cover it.

That evening fireworks were noisily appreciated by a quarter of a million on the river front, among them purse snatchers and pickpockets who had escaped being rounded up before the events. The display lit up the skyline, reminiscent of the effects of tracers and rockets fired by the gunships and fighter-bombers we used to watch from our grandstand, on top of the Caravelle Hotel, now renamed the Doc Lap (Freedom). Liberation Day was an anticlimax, lost to the hype that the media had injected into the Vietnamese, who had turned it around to hype themselves.

The meanings of this celebration and that going on in Europe were getting lost. The Germans, who had lost their war, were surfing high in plenty; the Vietnamese, who had theoretically won theirs, were still bogged down in a quagmire of desolation. Both nations composed of dedicated hard-working people, both overtly nationalistic, both reduced to ruin by war. One aided and now rich, the other ostracized and impoverished. The disparity is nowhere more apparent than in the state of the crippled war veterans. A few schools for blind vets, inadequate clinics producing prosthetics, or providing therapy; most amputees, both military and civilian, end up begging, or at best surviving on the very fringes of society. They number probably three-quarters of a million. No one has even bothered to calculate the number of war-related mentally afflicted; you see countless shell-shocked individuals the length of the country, but mostly in the southern provinces, where millions of old-regime troops are the nearest thing to State slaves. Those that can, try to escape on boats, or via the ODP (Orderly Departure Programme), thence to become refugees. Hundreds of thousands have left the country since liberation, to suffer afresh at the hands of pirates, or from the governments of the countries where they eventually land.

This photographer will be haunted for ever by the countless blind seen on the streets up and down this twisted land. Blindness is the crime that the various colonial dynasties have shown themselves and, viciously, perpetrated on the conquered. To the Vietnamese, the goal had been the ultimate, the most expensive—Liberation. A reflection of what Emperor Le Loi had written after organizing their release from the chains of the Ming dynasty. "Every man on Earth ought to accomplish some great enterprise, so that he leaves the sweet scent of his name to later generations. How, then, could he willingly be the slave of foreigners?" That was 1418—now the handcuffs are bejeweled with roubles.

Former re-education camp, now a holiday resort near Dau Tieng.

Bru Montagnard, Khe Sanh.

OPPOSITE
**Dak Lak provincial elephant
races in the Olympic Stadium,
Buon Me Thuot.**

**Memorial service at the
Military Cemetery, Xuan Loc,
after Tet.**

Couple whose son is in the
U.S. living in the ruins of the
home commandeered by
ARVN Marines in '72 as their
battle HQ.

The former bars of Tu Do (now Dong Khoi) Street, Ho'ville.

**Ex-Vietcong watching the
10th Anniversary of
Liberation parade.**

**Legless Bo Doi returning from
Kampuchean front, at the
Vinh Long Mekong ferry.**

**Near Moc Chau on the road to
Dien Bien Phu.**

Army on maneuvers, Dong Mo near Lang Son on the Chinese border.

OVERLEAF
Defoliation in the Mang Yang Pass on Route 19 from Qui Nhon to Play Cu.

Buddha destroyed in '72 offensive. An Loc.